PRAISE FOR *DON'T GET SUCKERED*

"I found *Don't Get Suckered* to be engaging because of Josh's personal story, informative because of all of his research, and inspiring because of the encouragement for those coming into their college years. Wow! Very well done! Every high school junior should be required to read *Don't Get Suckered*."

Dan Miller
Author of *48 Days to the Work You Love* and *No More Dreaded Mondays*
Franklin, Tennessee

"After witnessing countless young people hamstrung by enormous college debt, I am glad that someone is finally saying "Enough!" Josh's book is a preemptive strike that could enable the next army of young people to live out their destiny in God. We will certainly be using this in our church."

Robert Herber
Lead Pastor - All Peoples Church
San Diego, California

"It is refreshing to read simple truth; because the greatest truth is usually simple. Learn it, plan it, do it! That's simple enough to understand quickly and yet profound enough to change the circumstances of your life. We owe a 'debt' of gratitude to young men like Josh who are bringing uncommonly common sense to a generation who will inherit the mistakes of their fathers."

Bill Spencer
President – Narrow Gate Foundation
Franklin, Tennessee

"If you want to get out of college without debt, or if you want your child to start their life after college free from debt...you HAVE to read this! This project is more of a guide/workbook than any thing else and as it's practical instruction is implemented, you will find this to be one of the best investments you will ever make into your or your child's future."

Patrick Murphy
Pastor of Donor Ministries – Antioch Community Church
Waco, Texas

"I wish I had read this book before I went to college. It is filled with so much insight, practical help, and encouragement that it is doable to live a debt free life, even in college! I had the privilege of being Josh's friend and roommate at Baylor and know that Josh lived out what he writes. He is wise man and a hard worker. "

Joel Sanders
Awaken College Pastor
San Diego, California

DON'T GET
SUCKERED

HOW TO SURVIVE **COLLEGE DEBT FREE**

AND WITH YOUR SHIRT

JOSH LAWSON

*Disclaimer: The opinions found in this book are those of the author and do not necessarily reflect those of Antioch Community Church. This book is designed to provide accurate and authoritative information with regard to the subject matter covered; however, it does not replace financial, accounting, or other professional advice.

The names of some individuals whose stories are told in this book have been changed to protect their privacy.

Cover design by Kyle Rogers.

DEDICATION

This book is dedicated to my beautiful bride and best friend - Jennifer Nicole Lawson. Without your constant love, support and prayers, I would not be the man I am today. You have encouraged me when I have needed it (which is everyday) and made fun of me when I have taken myself too seriously (which is all too often). Thank you for continuing to push me forward with your encouragements and affirmations when I would too easily become overwhelmed and I wimp out. I love you with all that I am. Thank you for always being there with open arms and a beautiful smile.

CONTENTS

ACKNOWLEDGMENTS

I would be a fool not to acknowledge the multitude of people who have helped me in this journey to actually seeing the dream of publishing become a reality. Thank you Kerry, Noah, Caleb, Ryan, Zach, Steven, Jenny, and Mom, for giving me guidance since the beginning of this process. Thank you Zach and Vanessa, Kerry, Jordan, Robert, Courtney, Chelsea, and Dad for allowing me to use your stories so that others can be free. Joel, you're the man! Justin and Kyle, you two are pure geniuses. Thank you for all your help throughout the design process. For all my friends on 48days.net, thank you for taking the time to give me some great feedback and constructive criticism. Thank you to my family and friends in the Antioch Movement for loving Jesus and giving a young kid a safe place to learn and grow. And most importantly, thank you Lord Jesus for loving me and setting me free from a great debt that I could never repay. I love you.

FOREWORD

In the mid-1980's my wife, Laura, and I attended Baylor University. We graduated in 1986 and had the joy and privilege of walking out of college debt free. This was due in part to the support of our parents as well as our own determination to work hard for any extras that we might need. This allowed us to step out of college and dream and experience the dreams of God because we weren't bound by any extra obligations.

It has been a personal passion, as well as a personal commitment for Laura and me to live debt free so that at any day and at any moment we can move with the dreams of God. We desire that same passion and freedom for all of God's people and especially for college students. Over the last twenty-five years of ministry, I have had the privilege of working with thousands of college students, many of whom have graduated with great dreams but were unable to experience them because they were shackled by debt. As we have made different attempts to help people learn how to walk through college debt free, we have had some successes, but not nearly as many as are needed.

When I met Josh Lawson, I found he was also a dreamer. He was a man who wanted to be free to live out the big dreams of God. Early out of college, he connected with a close friend and they initiated with our church's leadership team to see if we would be interested in starting a ministry to help see people set free financially and ultimately come to know Jesus. We talked and prayed together and we said "absolutely." Josh and his friend had talked about starting a separate organization, but I admonished them that," this is what the church should be doing. You don't need to set-up a separate organization, we simply need to embrace you and partner together."

Josh began implementing this new ministry with a very familiar tool, Dave Ramsey's *Financial Peace University*, and over the past several years they have seen close to two million dollars in debt eradicated. Josh's passionate heart has continued to bleed out into our surrounding community as he has led the charge to see the poor and oppressed in our city lifted up.

One of my favorite phrases is, "live simply so that others might simply live." I believe this phrase is a perfect description of Josh and Jenny's life and testimony. Josh is not just a dreamer who is excited about his own life being free from debt, but he and his wife have continued to sacrifice and live the narrow life so that others can be set free. He has learned that life is not only about dreaming, but about applying truth in a very intentional, specific, and biblical way. I have been committed, as a pastor and teacher through communication and discipleship, to instill these same truths. Through Josh's book I now have a written piece to empower and help people live out their dreams.

In _Don't Get Suckered,_ Josh has been able to capture both the life-changing truth and the specific practicals and present them in a succinct and understandable way. This book is not only a series of stories of people who have struggled with and overcome debt by working through college, but it is a specific, practical guide for how you can do it too.

Imagine with me for a minute a growing revolution of young men and women, who are equipped with great faith and a manual in their hands. They are ready to launch out of college free from debt and free to say "YES" to the dreams of God. I believe this book is that practical manual and I am thrilled about the potential that it holds.

My prayer is that it would stir you, encourage you, and set you free to dream and pursue the big dreams of God. I encourage you to pass it on to a hundred, and even a thousand others. May we not just imagine but may we see that growing revolution of young people free from debt and free to pursue the dreams of God unshackled.

- Jimmy Seibert
Senior Leader Antioch Community Church and Antioch Ministries International

PREFACE

For the past eight years, my wife and I have had the opportunity to be a part of an amazing church in Waco, Texas called Antioch Community Church and for the past three years I have served as the director of the Financial Restoration Ministry.

The mission of our ministry is to see financial hope restored to people from every economic status- from the college student to the millionaire. We work to see people in our church, our community, and the nations of the earth set free from materialism, debt, and poverty, so that they are free to say "yes" to the plans God has for them.

In our church there are hundreds of young people who are fresh out of college and are starting their careers and families. Many of these young people often come from wealthy families where there seems to be no end to the bank account. If you want something, you get it. And if you don't get it quickly enough, you just have to whine long enough and loud enough and you will eventually get it.

We are little babies stuck in the bodies of a grown adult.

I like to call this the "spoiled brat mentality." Many of us have taken this mentality into college and our adult lives, and the consequences have been severe.

The "spoiled brat mentality" rears its ugly head in several different forms. It can look as simple as someone thinking that they deserve to buy a new toy even though they don't have the money, or as harmful as someone not taking responsibility for their actions and always blaming someone else.

I honestly cannot tell you how many times I have talked with someone who is in debt up to their eyeballs and they say to me, "Josh, I can't do anything about it, my parents were bad with money, and they never taught me how to handle it properly."

Stories from a Tightwad

Thankfully for me, my dad was just the opposite. He learned from the mistakes of others, and he swore to himself and his family that he would be good, no, great with money.

When my dad graduated from college he went to work for one of the big four accounting firms – Ernst and

Whinney. He was making great money, but life would soon throw him a curveball.

For several years my dad's mom had been consistently mentoring a young lady from her church. This young lady had recently come out of a horrific marriage and was now a single mom with three kids all under the age of five.

One day my dad's mother called him up and said, "Vance, I found your wife, only thing is she has three tax benefits." My dad laughed, but inside knew his mom was serious. Dad decided to humor his mom and he gave the young lady a phone call to see if there was anything there worth pursuing. Fortunately for me, there was.

One year later, my mom and dad tied the knot, and my dad went from being a young bachelor making great money with few expenses to a father of three wondering how he could make ends meet. He was forced to be great with money because everyone was depending on him, including his new family of five.

The Cheapest Man on Earth

It has been almost thirty years now and my parents are still debt free to this day. One of the main reasons they have remained debt free with such a large family is that my dad is a "tightwad." Many people in our family and circle of friends know him as the cheapest man on earth.

For instance, when I was in high school, my dad drove a 1991 baby-blue Cadillac, when it wasn't cool to drive a 1991 baby-blue Cadillac. In my mind it was the ugliest car

I had ever seen. His car reminded me of the old jalopy John Candy's character drove in the movie *Uncle Buck* (except it didn't backfire as badly).

We lived in a nice suburb and I went to a private school, so you can imagine that pulling into the school parking lot next to all the brand new Lexus' and Range Rovers was absolutely mortifying for an insecure teenager. At that point in my life, the pressures of materialism pressed hard on me and I would sink down in the passenger seat hoping no one would see me in the car and plead with my dad to sell the car.

My dad would always say, "As long as it gets me from point A to point B, I'm going to keep driving it." Thankfully, a little while later the engine exploded on its way to point B and it was finally time for dad to buy a new car. But to the horror of me, my family, and anyone who knew my dad, he decided to save the money and buy my great-grandmother's 1985 Cadillac.

I thought his old Cadillac was ugly, but this thing was an absolute tank. No joke, it was around 25 feet long and had a horn that would put the Titanic's horn to shame. My dad loved it though, mostly because it made us all cringe when we had to go anywhere with him.

One day at work my dad was walking past the water cooler and overheard a guy saying, "Hey did you see Boss Hogg's car out in the parking lot?"

The other guy exclaimed, "No, that's Mr. Lawson's car! He makes more money than all of us. Why in the world is he driving that car?"

My dad smiled because what they didn't realize was that he was driving that car then so that when he was older he could drive whatever car he wanted to.

The story gets even better. A few months after purchasing the 1985 land yacht, my dad was in an accident on the highway on his way to work. The other car slammed into the driver's side of my dad's car, crushed the door, and left black marks all down the side (imagine the wall at a NASCAR racetrack).

We all thought and prayed that this was officially the end of the Cadillac era. But, no, my dad continued to drive that car every day to and from work even though he had to climb in through the passenger door to get to the driver's seat.

At that time in my life, I was humiliated by my dad's frugality, but more and more I realize now that I am slowly turning into my dad. You always hear young guys say that statement and it's usually in a bitter tone, but you know, I am actually grateful.

My dad has never been impressed with material possessions and has never really been caught up in trying to keep up with the Joneses. He always jokes, "I've met the Joneses and they look good on the outside, but inside they are broke and miserable."

Looking back, I am thankful for the way my dad sacrificed so much so that our family could have the things in life that really mattered. What I didn't know in high school was that the money that my dad wasn't spending on new cars to make him *look* important was actually going to save up for his children's college education.

Without knowing it, he was teaching me the principles that I would eventually carry into my college and young adult years to help hundreds of people become financially free.

-**Josh Lawson**

INTRODUCTION

Baseball Dreams

My journey to college actually started when I was a small boy. Ever since I was a little boy, I can remember dreaming of playing professional baseball. To me there was no other option than playing baseball at the professional level and college was simply a step in the process to get there.

My entire life revolved around this dream of making it to the next level of baseball success. I started playing baseball when I was three years old, and played every year until I was eighteen.

Once I reached high school, the majority of my summer days were spent on the baseball diamond playing in league games, traveling to state and regional tournaments, attending "showcases" for college and professional scouts, and spending countless hours in a batting cage with a hitting coach.

However, as in all things, history tends to repeat itself and just like dad, life threw me a curveball.

Toward the end of my junior year I developed a severe pain in my bicep. I continued to play through the pain for the rest of that year, but by the spring of my senior season it started to feel like someone was drilling a hole through my bicep. Almost every time I would make a throw from the outfield, pain would shoot down my arm, it would go numb, and I would lose all strength. The pain became unbearable.

Reluctantly I decided to finally visit the local sports doctor, and after several MRI's he informed me that my rotator cuff was little by little coming unraveled. The years of playing baseball had put so much strain on my shoulder that it was starting to wear out. At that moment the doctor told me the news that no baseball player ever wants to hear, "Josh, it looks like you won't be able to play baseball for the rest of this year and potentially ever again."

It was at that point that I realized that my plan for my life had been taken captive. Baseball was my life. When I dreamed about my future, it was the only thing I could imagine. I never even had a plan B.

Therefore, I took some time and prayed long and hard about whether I should get shoulder surgery, sit out a year and then play at a Junior College, or just hang up my cleats and attend college strictly for the education. It was the hardest decision of my life, but after months of prayer I knew that I had to choose to go to school for the education.

The College Journey Began

During my childhood whenever our family would travel to see my grandparents in Gatesville, Texas, we would always stop by Waco and visit the beautiful Baylor campus or go to a Baylor football game. Even though I hadn't lived in Texas for 10 years, I had many fond memories of the state and always considered myself a Texan at heart. When I started looking at colleges, I knew that I wanted to get back to Texas and Baylor seemed like the best and most familiar option. I decided to apply and to my surprise was accepted.

I think it took my dad a few days to fully digest that announcement. In a matter of weeks, he went from having four years of college totally paid for through a baseball scholarship to now having to pay for Baylor University, one of the more expensive schools in the country.

The Cost of College

When you're in high school, life is fairly free from the challenges of finances. You don't really have a whole lot of expenses except going to the movies or maybe paying for gas. As I entered my freshman year at Baylor, I was clueless about the cost of college.

In college, everything has a price tag including the "wake me up" coffee in the morning, the 8x8 concrete box known as a dorm "room," and especially the overpriced textbooks that the publishers always seem to conveniently add a "new and improved" edition each semester.

At the beginning of my freshman year, my parents and I sat down and set the expectations for how all of these expenses would be handled.

It went a little like this: my first year my parents would pay for all living and school expenses. After that, it would be up to me to cover extracurricular activities. After my freshman year, my parents would begin handing off more and more expenses to me until I was financially independent by the time I graduated.

As my parents continued to explain the plan, I began hearing the Ka-ching of a cash register blaring in my brain. All I saw was dollar signs.

When my parents were paying for everything, it was like there was no end to money supply. Hopelessness began to sink in as I suddenly realized that I didn't have an endless bank account. My bank account had an end and it was closer than I wanted it to be.

If my parents weren't going to pay for everything, then that meant I had to find some way to cover several thousands of dollars worth of expenses each year. It meant that I would have to do the unthinkable. It meant that I would have to get a job! My inner spoiled brat was going crazy!

From that point on, whatever I made during the breaks from school was all that I had to spend that next semester. I had to become one of those beings that I dreaded growing up – an adult.

A Lifesaving Concept

Sometime during my junior year I heard about a concept called "budgeting." I had heard of these things before, but I thought they were only for big businesses or tightwads like my dad. However, being the competitor I am, I decided to give it my best shot. By the end of my junior year, my computer was filled with excel spreadsheets of pie graphs, projections, and budgets of how I was going to use my money that I had earned the previous break.

By the time I graduated from college, I was actually able to pay my final tuition bill with my own money and graduate from Baylor University debt free.

A year later, using the budgeting skills that I had learned while in school, I was able to purchase an engagement ring and pay for a honeymoon all without going into debt. I can proudly say that my wife and I are still completely debt free and one of the main reasons is that old guy who helped me silence my inner spoiled brat by driving that beat-up 1985 Cadillac and forcing me to work and pay for my college.

A Rare Story

As I have shared my story with countless high school and college students, I have realized that, sadly, my story is a rare one. Each year there are tens of thousands of young people who are making decisions about how to pay for college without anyone there to tell them how to make it through college debt free.

They don't have a dad teaching them what it looks like to live simply and work hard. They don't have someone teaching them how to do a budget. And more importantly they don't have someone helping them silence their inner spoiled brat.

This book is for that generation.

1
THE NARROW ROAD

Gloom is in the Forecast

The headlines of our nation's top newspapers and magazines paint a dismal picture for college students. "Students Suffocate under Tens of Thousands in Loans," declares the USA Today newspaper.

The statistics are staggering, too. According to the Project on Student Debt, among students who borrowed money for college, the average debt load was $24,000 for those students who graduated in 2009. Despite the recent economic downturn, that average debt load has increased 6% from previous years.

With the current condition of our economy, the future doesn't look bright for these new college graduates who are carrying such a large debt load. According to the Current Population Survey, which is provided by the Bureau of Labor and Statistics, the unemployment rate for recent college graduates increased from 5.8 percent in 2008 to 8.7 percent in 2009.

The high debt average and high unemployment rate among recent graduates combine to make a lethal concoction that leads to the most shocking statistic: according to the USA Today, 19% of Americans between the ages of 18-24 declared bankruptcy in 2001. What many of these young people don't realize is that bankruptcy rarely nullifies your student loan debt.

Oftentimes a student loan is simply the beginning of a debt-filled life. Young adults become acquainted with the debt system early in their lives so they begin to feel more comfortable taking on more debt in the form of credit cards, auto loans, and home mortgages, as they grow older.

Zach and Vanessa's Story

I have had countless conversations with young professionals who are overwhelmed with their debt load. Let me introduce you to one of those couples: Zach and Vanessa. This young couple met when they were juniors in college. It was puppy love at first sight. They both came from very different backgrounds. Zach was a military kid whose dad is a Chief Master Sergeant in the Air Force, while Vanessa grew up just outside of Los Angeles in a wealthy suburban community.

Coming out of high school, Zach had been offered a scholarship to play basketball at a small college in West Texas. Meaning he would get to live his dream of playing college basketball, but with the special perk of the university paying for all of his college expenses.

However, by the end of his freshman year, the honeymoon was over and he decided to transfer to Baylor. The decision to make the move to Baylor was a tough one for Zach. He had worked his entire life to earn a basketball scholarship so that he could attend college debt free, however, by transferring to Baylor he would be responsible for all of his college costs.

Leaving the scholarship behind, he drove to the Baylor campus in Waco, Texas; first stop, the financial aid office. After filling out a novel's worth of paperwork, he was set. Set with thousands of dollars of student loan debt. His adventure at Baylor had begun, and so had his adventure with a burden much larger than he knew at the time.

A Burden to Carry

Throughout his time in college, Zach was clueless about the debt that was accruing. However, as he entered his senior year, he began to realize that within a year he would have to begin paying on his student loans. He decided it would be a good idea to see how much debt he had managed to rack up the past four years.

As he gathered all different loans together, he began to add up all the figures using a calculator on his desk. As he input the final loan amount and pressed enter on the calculator, his heart sank. To his dismay the number on the calculator screen was a little over $115,000.

At that moment it was as if someone dropped a ten pound bag of sand on his chest. His mind began to race with questions like, "How in the world will I pay all of this back?" "Am I still going to be paying for my college when my kids are going to school?" "Was all this really worth it?" Finally, he asked the most pressing question yet, "How in the world am I going to tell Vanessa?"

His relationship with Vanessa was progressing along and he knew that she was definitely going to be the one for him. But was it fair to have her carry this burden with him? Vanessa didn't have any school debt, so how could he ask her to feel the same weight that he felt right now when she had done nothing wrong?

He decided to go ahead and tell her, but over the next few years, the debt was always in the forefront of Zach's mind. It was all that he thought about, talked about, prayed about, and worried about. As Zach and Vanessa's relationship progressed through dating, engagement, and ultimately marriage, it was also at the forefront of their relationship. It was all they talked about, prayed about, worried about, and, more importantly, fought about.

Vanessa had to choose not to become bitter about this debt even though she hated it with everything inside of her. She knew that it wouldn't help to beat Zach up for taking on the loans, and the best thing she could do would be to help him carry the load.

So after school and marriage, they were both forced to take jobs that were not ideal, but were necessary for them to pay off the debt faster.

At times it felt like they would never be free from the weight of the debt. At times they felt like it would stretch their marriage to the breaking point. But, thankfully, Zach and Vanessa are part of wonderful Christian community and they both have a thriving relationship with Jesus.

So although the past few years have been extremely difficult, they have drawn closer to one another and to Jesus through the process. They have chosen to confide in close friends of their struggles with the debt and those friends have helped carry some of the weight of the debt through prayer and encouragement. That is not the story for many who are in their same position.

House on My Back

Several years back a guy came into my office for a financial coaching session and as soon as he walked in the door I could see the lack of hope and despair in his eyes. Over the next couple of hours he began to share his story of how he had accumulated well over $150,000 in student loan debt and this debt load was ruining his life.

At one point he looked me in the eyes and said, "Josh, I feel like I'm carrying a house on my back all the time."

I looked him back in the eyes and said, "You pretty much are. You have the mortgage of a house; you just don't have the house to show for it."

When You Assume...

The basic problem with debt and especially student loans is that it is an assumption of the future. Many people will sign up for a ton of student loan debt when they are an 18 year-old, fuzzy-faced kid because they are expecting to land a job that pays over $50,000 when they graduate.

Problem is, dreams are called dreams for a reason, - they aren't reality. There is no 100%, sure-fire guarantee on the future. That's why you see so many twenty-two year-olds pulling their hair out as graduation creeps closer and they begin applying to anywhere and everywhere because Google hasn't called them yet for that top executive job.

Now, I am all for going to school to get a better education to enhance your opportunity for a better job in the future, but you should never assume that you will be able to land whatever job you want just because you get an expensive piece of paper.

I have met countless brilliant young people who decided to go to school to get a degree in a field where they thought they could for sure land a job as soon as they graduated. But for whatever reason, they didn't land that job and their assumption on the future eventually caught up with them.

Don't Get Suckered

You see, they have been suckered. You have been suckered. I have been suckered. We have been suckered to believe this little lie that debt is not that bad.

The excuses for taking on student loans are always the same. "Student loans are the only option for some people." "You realistically cannot go through a four-year school and not take out a student loan." "Student loan debt is considered a 'good debt.'" "Everyone has a little bit of debt, right?" "You have to have a diploma to land that job when you graduate." "Debt is just a normal part of life." I would beg to differ with each of these excuses. Actually, I wouldn't beg, I would just differ.

But who is it that keeps feeding our young people all of these lies? Well, it's the loan companies of course. The Federal Government and private banks know that if they can get you when you are young they will have you hooked for the rest of your life. So they make it easy to get started with a student loan and attend the college of your dreams. They say, "It's so easy. Just sign this line and you don't have to worry about a thing for four more years. It won't hurt at all, I promise."

My, what big teeth you have, grandma!

What they don't tell you is how hard the road will be once you leave college. It is the age-old truth that the road to hell is paved with daisies and lollipops. It all looks great and tastes great until you take a glance down the path and see where you're headed.

You might be thinking to yourself, "Oh come on, Josh, it's really not that bad! You're just overreacting and making it a bigger deal than it really is so you can sell more books."

Truth be told, I have met with too many young people who have cried countless tears as they shared their gut-wrenching stories for me to sit back and believe that the lies are true. It is a big deal and the plain and simple truth is that I am sick of it. I am sick of millions of young people being taken advantage of each year. I am tired of seeing my friends' marriages stretched to the breaking point because of debt. I hate seeing people even consider bankruptcy or much worse suicide because their payments are suffocating them. Something needs to change.

Two Roads

In the Bible in the Gospel of Matthew, Jesus talks about two different paths in life, "Enter through the narrow gate. For wide is the gate and broad is the road that leads to destruction, and many enter through it. But small is the gate and narrow the road that leads to life and only a few find it."

There is a principle here that is applicable to all areas of our life. The easy road is that way for a reason – because it leads to death. But the road that leads to life is narrow and only a few people go that way. Why wouldn't everyone decide to go that way? Because it's hard. And it's not fun.

But, I have a handful of friends who have done it. They have chosen to not believe the lie that debt is okay and they've decided go through college debt free. And they have all done it in several unique ways. This book is about those people and how they have done it. This book is about a handful of people who saw the daisies and lollipops for what they were and ran down a different path. They have chosen the narrow road.

The same is true for you on this journey of graduating college debt free. There are two paths before you. There is the easy path that seems painless, but in the end really isn't. And there is a narrow path that looks hard and really is hard, but in the end you will find life. I would encourage you to take that narrow path.

But please know that it won't be easy. It will be hard. You will have to work. You will have to get dirt underneath your finger nails. You will have to sweat. You probably won't be able to have as much fun as everyone else for a few years. You won't be able to go out to eat as much as your friends and you will have to work during the summers. But when you walk across that stage and shake hands with the president of your school and grab that diploma, you can smile from ear to ear knowing that you are a free man or woman and you can now have as much fun as you want.

So, please hear the voices of the thousands of people who have followed the daisy and lollipop way as they call out to you, "Don't Get Suckered!"

The Road Ahead

In the next few chapters we will outline three major principles for you to follow to help you stay on the narrow path. The principles of the narrow path are not a new craze or passing fad. Instead, they are proven, age-old truths that people have been following for years.

We will start by exploring how scholarships and grants are the foundation for your debt free journey. We will learn what it takes to earn them and where you can find the scholarships that fit you.

Next, we will discuss how to supplement your scholarships with income from good old fashioned hard work. We will explain where a college student can find work and what it takes to land that dream job or even start your own company.

Finally, we will end by discussing how you can avoid taking on even more debt by learning how to manage your money properly.

Throughout the next few chapters you will also hear stories from young people just like you who decided to go down that narrow path.

Are you ready?

The journey down the narrow path begins today.

2
WHO WANTS SOME FREE MONEY

FREE MONEY!!!

Let's say one day I started to feel a little bit crazy and began to run through the streets with a duffle bag full of money (that I just so happened to find) screaming, "Free money! Who wants some free money? I have a duffle bag full of thousands of dollars. Who wants some of it?" What do you think would happen?

People would initially think that I was on some kind of hard drug. But once they realized that I was serious and actually did have a duffle bag full of cash, I would most likely get absolutely mobbed. Literally. People would be chasing me down and doing whatever it took to get that free money from me. Why? Because people are desperate for some free money.

But each year, there are literally millions of dollars in both scholarships and grants that go unclaimed. Businesses, civic organizations, and even the federal government have duffle bags upon duffle bags full of money and they are screaming, "Free money! Who wants some free money?" But no one is taking it.

Do you want some free money? Of course you do. Do you need some free money? Most likely. So how do you get it? Or more than likely, you're asking yourself, "Can I really pay for college with scholarships?"

All your questions and even more will be answered in this chapter as you learn how to find enough free money to pay for education with scholarships.

You Need the Money

As the cost of college continues to increase, free money is the first major way for you to pay for college without taking out student loans. Each year there is over $3 billion in private scholarships that are awarded to college students. The average given away is $2,000 to $3,000 a year per student. Where does all this money come from?

The following are the main sources of scholarships:

- College endowments

- Corporations

- Non-profits – which include public interest groups, foundations, religious organizations and civic organizations

- And government agencies

In order to maximize your opportunity for receiving a scholarship, or multiple scholarships, from one of these sources, here are a handful of tricks of the trade to stick to.

1. The Early Bird Gets the Worm

Start applying for scholarships early. If you are just starting to apply for a scholarship in July and your freshman year starts in August, you're probably too late. The money is already gone. The early bird already got the worm.

The best way to earn a scholarship is by making great grades while you are in high school. This takes some forethought and planning, but understanding that many colleges will award you handsomely for excellent grades and test scores should be enough initiative for you to put in the hard work early on.

I would encourage you to start making a list of potential scholarships when you are a sophomore in high school. If there is a scholarship out there for someone who volunteers at the local soup kitchen during high school, well, you better get your hairnet ready!

Some schools actually give priority for scholarships to early decision and early action applicants. This means if you know where you want to attend school, go ahead and commit as soon as possible. This makes you more likely to get an early decision scholarship.

Also remember that it takes longer to apply properly for a scholarship than you think. In order to have a legitimate shot at getting a scholarship, you want to be sure and have essays that are grammatically correct and have been edited multiple times before you send them in.

2. Don't Waste Your Time

You will be a lot more productive if you focus your energy on scholarships that you have the greatest potential to get. If you aren't a pre-med major from Russia with blue eyes, there is no point in applying for that scholarship.

As you search through scholarships on the local, regional and national level, start by making a list of the ones that you have a higher probability of earning. Once you have organized this list, now you can focus more of your time and energy on preparing a top-notch application.

3.   A Penny a Day

Even the smallest scholarships can add up to a lot of money. Don't be afraid to apply for the smaller scholarships because you don't think it will help. Every penny will help you get a little bit closer to your goal of paying cash for college.

Researching scholarships and completing applications is often time-consuming but can result in large pay-offs. When I was going into college I saw scholarship searching as my full-time job. I wasn't being paid for it at the time but in essence I was earning thousands of dollars for all of my hard work.

An easy way to calculate how many scholarships you need is to back your way into it. Start by finding out how much each school year is going to cost. Be sure to include everything from textbooks to room and board. Now that you have that figure and you know that the average scholarship awarded is between two and three thousand dollars, simply divide the overall cost of your school by two or three thousand.

For instance, if your school will cost $30,000 each year, that means that you will need between ten and fifteen scholarships to pay for school if those scholarships are for all four years.

4. Leave No Stone Unturned

When I was growing up, I would go crawdad hunting. I know what you're thinking, "Isn't that what country boys do, Josh?" And yes it is, my friend. Every summer we would head down to the creek that ran behind our house, roll up our jeans, and start turning over every rock because that's where the crawdads hid. You didn't know which rock they would be hiding under, so you had to turn over each rock one by one until you found that Cajun beauty.

The same thing is true for the scholarship search process. There are thousands of scholarships hiding all over the place and your job is to roll up your jeans and find out where they are.

When starting the scholarship search process, be sure to take into account that there are several types of scholarships out there ranging from those awarded based on financial need to those awarded by your parent's company.

So if you are worried about your grades not being high enough, know that academic success is only one of the requirements for several scholarships.

Where Do You Find Scholarships?

School of Choice

The majority of significant scholarships are awarded to students by the school that they attend. These are usually the best known scholarships and therefore most sought after and most competitive. School based scholarships are given in different areas including: athletic, financial need-based, academic merit, and various other criteria.

When I was going into Baylor, there were certain scholarships that were automatically given for people who had certain GPAs or standardized test scores.

Often the best place to receive information about scholarships available from your school of choice is your school's website or directly from their financial aid office.

A few years ago, Jenny and I were meeting with a young lady who was about to start her first year of graduate school. She had already accrued a mountain of student loan debt from her undergraduate studies, but she had recently been through one of our classes and now wished to go through graduate school debt free.

At the time we met it seemed impossible because she was already working and living as simply as she could. We encouraged her to look for scholarships in her particular field of study.

A couple weeks later she came running up to us exclaiming that she had talked with one of her professors and it just so happened that the exact week we had talked a new scholarship had been opened for that department. She applied and was awarded the scholarship that would cover the rest of her graduate studies!

Then she said that the professor she had talked to actually wanted to hire her on as a graduate assistant. Within a matter of weeks, this young lady went from the only option for paying for school was to take on more debt, to now she was actually being paid to attend school.

Employers

If you are choosing to go back to school, keep in mind that many employers encourage their employees to further their education by either covering or supplementing their tuition costs. The majority of companies will more than likely increase your position and pay once your studies are finished.

I have had countless family members and friends receive either a full scholarship or full reimbursement from the company that they are currently working for. Employers often see this as an investment not just in the future of their employees but as an investment in the future of their company.

Even if you are graduating from high school, some companies have a scholarship program for the children of employees. Encourage your parents to check with their human resources director as you begin your scholarship search.

There is also the opportunity to work for a company part-time or during the summer that offers scholarships for its workers. For example, each year McDonald's awards an employee from each state with a scholarship ranging from $1,000 to $5,000.

Locally

Local scholarships are often a great option when you are starting out because they often tend to be less competitive because you are only competing against college students in your city or region rather than nation-wide or even internationally.

The best way to find these local scholarships is usually through your high school counselor. Ask them to help you research local scholarships and see if they can get you all the information you need: application, application due date, organization or company, etc.

Another way to find local scholarships is to speak with local businesses or civic organizations. If you know someone who is a business owner, ask them if their company gives any scholarships and how you would go about applying for it. Civic or religious organizations that you are affiliated with are another great place to look for local scholarships. If you are a part of a local church, ask your pastor if your church gives any scholarships.

Each year my wife's hometown church awards one high school graduate from their congregation a $1,000 scholarship.

Your State Department of Higher Education

If you are interested in attending an in-state college, most states have a scholarship program for their residents. For instance, in the state of Texas the top 10% of each high school graduation class has the opportunity to receive up to $2,000 in scholarship to a 2 year or 4 year state school.

When I lived in Tennessee, there was a scholarship known as the Hope Scholarship. If you met the requirements of this scholarship, you were awarded $1,000 each year for a Tennessee school. Several of my classmates used this scholarship to help pay for their college education.

Online Scholarship Search Tools

For many students, the task of actually finding a scholarship is a daunting one. Many students don't even know where to start. In years past in order to locate a handful of scholarships that fit your profile, you would have to spend hour upon hour scouring through hundreds of publications or reference books.

Luckily finding a scholarship that matches your profile is easier than ever due to the numerous scholarship search websites that help students find scholarships for which they are actually eligible.

These websites will ask you a set of questions and then using the information, they locate scholarships that may be appropriate for you.

Two of the best services that I have seen which have large databases of available scholarships and actually do a good job of matching scholarships to your profile are Fastweb.com and Kaarme's Scholarship Finder.

Avoid Scholarship Finder Scams

As you look to take advantage of scholarship search services, please keep in mind that there are several scholarships scams out there. A good rule of thumb when using these scholarship search services is, "if it seems too good to be true, then it probably is."

The scholarship scam industry has become so prevalent that the Federal Trade Commission has set-up a website to help inform students of what a scholarship scam might look like or sounds like.

The FTC cautions students to look for the following tell-tale lines of a scam:

"The scholarship is guaranteed or your money back."

"You can't get this information anywhere else."

"I just need your credit card or bank account number to hold this scholarship."

"We'll do all the work."

"The scholarship will cost some money."

"You've been selected by a 'national foundation' to receive a scholarship"

Or "You're a finalist" in a contest you never entered.

How to Apply for a Scholarship

Since there is such a great opportunity to pay for college using scholarships, you want to be sure and take the scholarship application process just as seriously as the actual college application process. You will be more successful if you go into this process seeing it as your job. Imagine that each scholarship you are awarded is simply a commission check that you get to cash in the near future.

Getting Started

Many of the scholarship applications ask for the same information, so before you even begin filling out your first application, be sure to create a folder with all of your information that will be needed for the applications. Many scholarships require you to provide some combination of the following:

- Standardized test scores
- Financial aid forms, such as the FAFSA or CSS/Financial Aid PROFILE®
- Parents' financial information, including tax returns
- Transcript
- One or more essays
- One or more letters of recommendation
- And proof of eligibility (e.g., membership credentials)

Be Honest

Once you have gathered all the information you need and start to fill out the application, remember to be honest.

It might be tempting to dress-up your application a little bit and make it seem like you are something you're not. You might think that you have a higher probability of earning that scholarship if you tell them you're an Eagle Scout, but honestly, who wants to lie about being an Eagle Scout.

Be true to yourself through this whole process, and if you have had some failures, don't be afraid to share those. You don't want to dwell on your failures, but you can use them to show how you have learned and matured through the process.

Details, Details, Details

You have probably heard it said before that the devil is in the details. I actually like to think that the victory is in the details. If you prepare and execute the details, victory is almost a sure thing. The same is true for the scholarship application process.

The victory for the scholarship application process is found in the details. Remind yourself as you begin the process of applying for scholarships that putting together a quality application could earn you thousands, if not tens of thousands, of dollars in scholarships. Be painfully thorough in the whole process.

Proofread Multiple Times

You can write the most compelling short essay, but if you have multiple spelling or grammatical mistakes it will immediately put you out of the running for the scholarship. Use your computer's spelling and grammar check features and have a family member, teacher, or friend read your essays.

Don't Leave Items Blank

If you aren't sure what a question is asking, go ahead and contact the scholarship sponsor or ask your parents or school counselor for clarity.

Follow Instructions to the Letter

Make a note of how long each of the essays should be and don't go over that length. Use your word count tool inside of your Microsoft Word document to double check this.

If the question asks for an in-depth essay of who your hero is, don't just give a one-line answer. Before you start to answer a question, read through the instructions twice and underline or highlight any pertinent details.

Always Double-Check

Often times you can send the same essay or cover letter for several scholarships; if this is the case be sure to double check all the information to ensure there is no overlap or wrong names.

The scholarship process can become tedious at times, but don't lose heart. Be sure to remain as detailed as you possibly can throughout the whole process. If your mind becomes cloudy, take a break and come back to the application later on.

Taking Care of the Gap

My junior year at Baylor I had the opportunity to meet and mentor one of the brightest young men I have ever met. He was the kind of guy that makes you sick because he never has to study and still has a perfect 4.0 G.P.A.

Before his freshman year he was awarded a major academic scholarship that paid for about 99% of his college expenses. The only trouble was that he still had a couple thousand dollars each year that he would have to cover.

Instead of just looking at his predicament and deciding to take the easy road and get a loan for a couple thousand dollars, he chose to put in the hard work and apply for more scholarships. After everything was said and done, he was practically paid to go to school each year.

Retaining Earned Scholarships

Also remember, once you have received a scholarship, you want to make sure and do everything you can to retain that scholarship throughout your college years. If a scholarship requires a 3.0 GPA, then you better be doing everything you can to keep that grade point average.

How sad would it be to do all that hard work to be awarded a scholarship only to lose it because you decided to watch a little too much television or hang out with your friends instead of studying. Now I might sound like your dad here, but your education is the whole reason that you are going to this thing called "college."

I promise, your friends will still be there, and the people on television on that singing or dancing competition will survive without you watching them. Go ahead and crack open that $200 textbook and put in the hard work to make sure that you retain your scholarships.

It Is Worth It

I cannot emphasize enough how important scholarships are to the whole process of paying for college without using student loans. You will not regret putting in the long hours of research to find the best scholarships or putting together a winning scholarship application. It might be hard right now, but in the end it will be worth it.

So go ahead and chase down those guys with the duffle bags full of free money.

3
PAYING FOR COLLEGE WITH SWEAT

Obviously the best place to start when you are looking for a way to pay for college is scholarships and grants. This money is free and awarded according to who you are, what you are currently doing, and what you have accomplished.

Simple.

All you have to do is put in a little leg work and you could have a large portion of your college expenses covered, if not the entire amount.

But what if there is still some left over? Who pays for you to have fun on the weekends? What about getting gas for your car?

If you're anything like a normal 18 to 22 year-old in America, you will really not like what I am about to say. You need to get a job. That's right a good old fashioned J.O.B. It might sound like a foreign idea, but I promise you people have been working since the dawn of creation.

Go Be a Bookseller

Let me introduce you to one of my good friends, Jordan. In his first year at a private university, he was clueless like many first time students and he took out $12,500 to get him through his first year. It was the rational thing for him to do because his parents weren't able to help with college. He tried to get as many scholarships as he possibly could, but there was still a good amount left to cover.

In looking back on the situation Jordan recalls, "I never even hesitated about the idea of applying for student loans. I just assumed that is what everybody did and I would pay them off after college when I landed my entry level six-figure job...no big deal."

Direction from a College Pastor

It sounds all too familiar. But thankfully he would not end college the same way that many students do. One day while talking with his college pastor about his school loans, his college pastor encouraged him to pray for a way to be able to pay for school without taking out any more loans.

That statement from his college pastor caught Jordan off guard. Jordan thought to himself, "It's impossible to graduate college without student loans! There was no way that a college kid could make $12,000 by working during college." As those thoughts ran through his mind, Jordan was interrupted by his college pastor asking him to pray.

He gave a half-hearted prayer which mentioned something about asking God for help to find some way to pay for school. As soon as Jordan said "amen" a guy walked up to their table and began to tell them his story of how he had made over $12,000 the previous summer selling books door to door.

In case you were wondering, the word "amen" actually means "let it be." In this case God "let it be" for Jordan a little bit sooner than he was expecting.

That next summer Jordan began selling books door to door and in his first summer he made a little over $10,000. He decided this book selling idea actually worked, so he continued to keep selling books summer after summer and each year he made more than the first.

He was able to never take out another loan again and by the time he walked across the stage his senior year, he was able to pay off his loan he took out his freshman year.

Jordan recalls his college experience by exclaiming, "I didn't realize what a burden $60,000 to $80,000 in debt would have been for me just starting out life after college! I wanted to be able to be free to go anywhere and do anything that the Lord put on my heart, and not be tied down to paying off this debt for years to come. I am so thankful to have been free from the weight and burden of debt after graduation. I was able to travel to Europe, go on several mission trips, and even spend an extended season of my life working in Sri Lanka after the tsunami hit."

Pain Now... or Pain Later

There are countless other stories of people who have graduated college debt free by working, but the common thread throughout all of them is that each person chose to give up a little pleasure in the short term so that they could be free from debt in the long term. Many college students don't realize the long term ramifications of taking out a student loan. And by the way, work seems too hard. It seems like... work. And college should be fun, right?

Let me say it another way. You could either work your tail off for four years while you are in college, or you could have a fun, care-free time during school but end up having to work your tail off for the next 30 years to pay for school.

I could tell you countless stories of people who have chosen jobs that they absolutely hate in a town that is hundreds of miles away from their friends and family just because the job pays enough for them to cover their student loan payments.

And by the way, work doesn't always have to be a drag. Of course you always see in the movies a young person working hard while all their friends head off to the lake. But what the movies don't show is that many of those people who are working hard while their friends are playing are actually having a great time.

Many of the people that I have talked to who worked during college have said that they met some of their life-long friends at those jobs. And who wouldn't have fun when you are pulling in about three to four thousand dollars a month while you're still in school?

What Kind of Person Are You?

Besides just the benefit of helping you become debt free, working in college does so much more for you. There is this little thing called character that is shaped while you are in college. If you choose to work during college, your character is being developed, and gradually you will become a person who is hardworking, diligent, faithful, trustworthy, and responsible.

Now, I am going to say something that might offend you and make you a little annoyed or uneasy, but it must be said. The purpose of you going to college is not to have a ton of fun and gain dozens of new friends. Those are all great, but they are secondary to the real purpose of your college education, which is to get you ready for your "adult life." Your college years are a training ground for what you will do and who you will be in the future. One of the best ways to develop your character and get you ready for your future is to work.

What Do Employers Really Look At?

As I have talked with business owners over the years, they have told me that one of the major things that they look for in a job applicant is work history. They really don't care too much if you went abroad to England and studied physics. They are more concerned with finding out if you are the kind of person who would be a benefit to their company and that they would like to have around their offices.

One of the quickest ways for employers to find this out is to look at your work history. Were you faithful to work? Were you a great employee? Do you even have a work history? Or did you even start your own company?

Start Your Own Company

When I encourage college students to get a job while in school, the first thing many of them think about is flipping burgers at a greasy burger barn or working at the local coffee shop. While these jobs can be fun and semi-useful, a better opportunity to make more money and learn more skills would be to start your own company.

You probably won't start the next mega million dollar company, but maybe you could (a guy named Bill Gates started a small company called Microsoft while he was in college). On the whole entrepreneurs make more money than a part time minimum wage worker.

Take a look at figure 3.1. Imagine you have to decide whether or not you should work at the local Greasy Burger Barn or start your own company. At the Greasy Burger Barn, you can make quick and easy money, but by the end of the summer, you will only have made around $3,600, which will probably cover your textbooks for this next year.

Or you could decide to start your own business like a landscaping company. On average you can earn about $60 an hour mowing yards, but let's just say you decide to charge a little bit less since you are just starting out. If you only ran your landscaping business for the three months of the summer, you would end up making over $14,000. That is four times what you would have made at the local Greasy Burger Barn.

Figure 3.1			
Entrepreneurship vs. Minimum Wage			
	# of Hrs. Worked During Summer	Amount Earned per Hour	Total Income Before Taxes
Starting Your Own Landscaping Business	480	$30	$14,400
Hourly Minimum Wage Job	480	$7.50	$3,600
		Difference	$10,800

Without a doubt starting your own company will take more personal drive and energy and effort, but again in the end, the payoff is much greater.

One of my good friends, Ryan, decided to take this route and be an entrepreneur. While he was in college, he started several companies ranging from gum ball machines to a t-shirt company. These companies weren't extremely profitable, but he made enough to help pay for college and he learned a great deal about business in the process.

When the time came for Ryan to graduate college, he was approached by a local real estate broker in town to become a real estate agent. During his time in college, he had proved his ability to sell and market his ideas and this was perfect preparation for his new position. Today Ryan continues to be a successful entrepreneur and he attributes much of his success to the lessons he learned while running those small companies while in college.

If you do decide to start your own company, start with something that you have a passion for or a unique skill in. If you love playing baseball, why don't you start training younger baseball players? Or if you love being outdoors, why not start a lawn mowing company?

God has created each of us with a unique set of skills and abilities and He wants us to express those through our work. There is an old saying that if you do what you love, then you will work harder at it. And if you work harder at it, then you will make more money doing it. And if you make more money at it, then you will love it even more.

One of my favorite resources on the subject of work and starting your own businesses is *48 Days to the Work You Love* by Dan Miller. You can find more information on his website – www.48days.com.

My Own Personal Story

When I was in college, I had about ten different jobs ranging from stuffing envelopes to selling kitchen knives. Every Christmas and summer break I would head back home and work every hour I could. It was actually really good for me to work.

As a young man, probably the worst thing that I could have done during the breaks is to go home and not work. I would have more than likely played on the Xbox360 for ten hours a day, stayed up until 4 AM, and then slept until noon.

It would have built a lazy bone in me. But instead I worked 40 hour a week like a "big boy" and it built in me a deep work ethic, one that I took with me into my adult years.

While I was in college, I read a book by Tommy Nelson in which he described the meaning of the word character. He said that in the Old Testament character can be translated as "carving, or etching, on a stone." As I read those words, something in my mind clicked and I realized that the character that I developed while in college would be carved in to the stone of my soul forever. In my minds eye I saw a sculptor, like Michelangelo, with a hammer and chisel carving a huge piece of marble.

I realized that if I chose to be lazy while I was in college, then that would be the sculpture that I became. Laziness would be etched deep into my soul. On the other hand, if I chose to be hardworking, then that would be the statue that I would become and integrity would be etched deep into my being.

The good news is that you are young enough now to choose what you want etched into your soul. There is still time to change what is being carved!

Be Excellent in Your Work

Whichever way you decide to go, whether working an hourly job or starting your own company, I encourage you to give it your all. Don't hold anything back. Show up to work early and work late. Learn everything that you can about business and how to work with other people. Some of the greatest lessons I have ever learned about work and working with other people, I learned during those summer and Christmas breaks.

I remember one Christmas break I was working as an intern at a company in Nashville. One day while I was working, this guy saw how hard I was working and he came up to me and said, "Whoa, whoa, whoa. Josh, you need to settle down, man. If you keep working this hard, there won't be any work left for you, man. You need to take it easy and spread this work over an entire week." I smiled and nodded then went right back on working.

Later on that day I jokingly told my boss about what the guy had said. What I didn't realize was that the guy had been hired by the company as a contract worker, meaning he was there as long as his talents were still needed. Needless to say, his talents were not needed anymore after that day.

Practice Makes Permanent

When I was young, I had a baseball coach who during every single practice would say, "Practice makes permanent, boys, practice makes permanent." After a while it became a resounding gong, but it has continued to stick in my head to this day. He turned the usual "practice makes perfect" phrase around because practice doesn't really make perfect.

No matter how much you practice, you will never truly be perfect, but practice does make permanent. How you practice today and tomorrow will become permanent in your life.

If you ever see a basketball player who makes a high percentage of their free throws, it is usually because they have spent countless hours in the gym shooting thousands upon thousand of free throws.

This past year I had the delight of watching my favorite basketball team, the Dallas Mavericks, win their first World Championship. They were led by Dirk Nowitzki, who even though he has some of the most unorthodox shooting habits, will most likely go down as the greatest 7-foot shooter in the history of the NBA.

During the playoffs the announcers would show Dirk before the game practicing in the gym with his trainer. He was doing all kinds of funky shots including shooting off of one leg while spinning and fading away. But then they showed these goofy looking shots side-by-side with shots that he was actually making during the game.

There is this amazing thing that happens in the human body after you repeat a movement several times called muscle memory. After several repetitions of a movement, your body stores that movement in its memory bank and you are able to perform it without a conscious effort in the future.

Dirk had practiced those unorthodox shots thousands of times for fifteen years until they had become a permanently memorized movement.

Every day you are practicing some type of muscle movement that is becoming a permanent part of your life. Whether that movement is laziness or hard work, as you continue to practice that movement over and over it will become permanent.

What you do now will affect your future. Hard work now will pay off later. Laziness now won't just disappear; it will always show up sometime in the future.

Choose today what you want your future to look like, and then begin to work to see that future become a reality.

4
LIVE ON A PLAN

During your time before college and even as a college student, one of the critical disciplines to learn is how to develop and implement a financial plan for your life. I have met with hundreds of people who would plead with you to start now living on a plan.

A few months back we took a poll of current college students ranging from fuzzy-faced freshman to nearly graduated seniors and asked them what they wished someone would teach them about finances. I was surprised when over half the students responded with budgeting as their number one answer. The thing is, young people really do want to learn how to be disciplined and how to budget, but few take the time or effort to learn how to do it until it actually hurts.

It's just like my decision in middle school to finally get braces. For years I hated the idea of taking a trip to a doctor to get my mouth jammed full of metal to make me look like Optimus Prime.

But eventually, the fear of that painful process paled in comparison to the painful thought of living the rest of my life with my two front teeth being an inch apart. It didn't really hurt for them to be an inch apart. What hurt was the insults and wisecracks that the other kids would throw my way.

For instance, one day while waiting for my parents to pick me up from school a kid came up to me and said, "Hey Josh, I don't know whether to smile back at you or kick a field goal."

Ouch. I decided at that moment that it was time for braces and I didn't really care what pain I had to go through.

I am going to save you the pain of many years of not living on a plan and explain in layman's terms how to do a budget so that you will be able to succeed financially both in college and outside of college.

The Most Important Formula, Ever

The most important formula that you will need to know when it comes to budgeting is:

Income – Outflow = 0

That's right, after everything is said and done, you need to have a big fat zero at the bottom of your page. This is what the financial experts call a "zero based cash –flow plan." After you subtract everything in your budget from your income, you want to be left with a zero at the bottom.

I can already hear you starting to grumble and complain, and I'm not too worried because I've heard it all before. It usually goes something like this, "I can't tell every dollar where to go, I need some flexibility in my life," or "Well, I don't want to be broke at the end of the month, and I need some left over."

If you don't plan what you are going to do with your leftover money, you will be broke and have zero flexibility!

Take this example: Go to the bank and get $200 out. Now go spend it on whatever you want for the rest of the month. Alright, it's the end of the month; now tell me what you did with that money.

You probably had some great ideas for what you wanted to do with that money. You probably wanted to save some of it or even give some it, but where did it all go?

See my point; you had no plan for what you were going to do with that money, so who knows where it went? I will guarantee you that more of it than you realize went to eating out or buying junk.

The truth is that is how we live our lives. Each month if we have a little bit leftover after our expenses are paid the majority of it will go right out the window. If you would have taken that $200 and had a plan for it, you could have been a lot more intentional with it and you probably could have done more with it. You could have saved more and given more like you wanted to.

Each month before you get the check from your parents or whoever you are working for, take out a piece of paper and do a simple cash flow plan. Write out all the income you will receive and then all of your expenses. On the next page is a sample budget to help you get started.

Figure 4.1	
TOTAL INCOME	
- TOTAL EXPENSES	
Tithes/Giving	
Savings	
Rent	
Renter's Insurance	
Electricity	
Gas	
Water	
Cable	
Cell Phone	
Groceries	
Eating Out	
Gas	
Car Payment	
Car Insurance	
Clothing	
Entertainment	
Other Misc.	
Other Misc.	
	= O

Keep It Simple

Usually someone in college has a pretty simple cash flow plan. It might include the following: Tithes, saving, rent, bills, gas, groceries, dining out, entertainment, and maybe a few others. Don't make your first budget too hard, there's no reason for it to be.

When I was in college, I was a nerd when it came to finances. I actually still am a nerd, but I was seriously a "pocket protector" kind of nerd. My computer was full of Excel documents where I tediously tracked each expense that I spent and any income that I received. I actually had pie charts to show what percentage I spent on different areas and even projections of my future income and expenses.

When Jenny and I first got married, I sat her down and showed her all of my spreadsheets. I was expecting her to be so proud of me, but she actually looked like she was about to throw up. As I continued to explain it all to her, she had this glazed look over her eyes and at the end of my presentation said, "You better make that a lot simpler or I'm not going to do it." Deflated I took out my yellow pad and tore out a piece of paper. I then wrote our income at the top and all of our expenses. That was our first budget as a couple.

Please don't put yourself through the same torture that I put myself and my wife through. It's really not worth it. Keep it really simple in college. All you really need each month starting out is one piece of paper from a yellow pad.

Should College Students Tithe

If you are making money in college, you need to be tithing. Some people would disagree with me on this, but my belief is that you should tithe on whatever your parents are giving you, if not only for the one reason that it gets you in the rhythm of consistently giving.

I have noticed that it helps the tithe become more concrete and understandable if you imagine your income as a field of corn. In biblical times and even today in some parts of the world, people would bring the first portion of their harvests to God and the local storehouse as a place of worship and thankfulness. This storehouse would go to help feed those in need and provide for the priests. The tithe was a mandate by God that encouraged the people to recognize God's ownership over everything.

Each month we work diligently and we produce a harvest known as money or income. The storehouse in today's time would be considered your local church since that is where you are worshipping and being equipped. As we produce a harvest, we are still encouraged to bring a percentage of that harvest to the local church. It doesn't matter if we have a small harvest or a large harvest; God invites us all to bring a tithe of our increase.

And in case you weren't sure, a tithe means a tenth, not just whatever change you have in your pocket on Sunday mornings. Biblically, God invites us to give the first fruits of our increase, so the tithe should be the first thing that you put on your budget. Honestly, if you wait until the end of the month to tithe, you won't do it.

When I was in college and starting to make money, I found myself complaining about having to give to God what I thought was such a big portion of my income. I expressed my frustration to a friend and he said, "Josh, if you can't live on 90%, then you probably can't live on 100%."

If you are having trouble with this idea, I would encourage you not to allow it to be a heavy or restrictive idea. The whole reason that God put it in place was to set us free from holding on too tightly to our material possessions. The God of the universe doesn't need your money, but He does want you to be free. Instead of the tithe becoming a place of duty or burden, let it become a place where you thank God for what you have been given.

Basic Necessities

After the tithe, the next item in your budget should be your basic necessities. The Bible encourages us to take care of our own household before we do anything else or we are worse off than an unbeliever. I don't even know what that means, but it scares me to death! So let's make sure and take care of our household's basic necessities before we take care of any other expenses.

The basic necessities in life can be broken down into four areas: housing, transportation, food and clothing. The first thing that you want to take care of is your housing. This can include rent payments or mortgage payments, utilities, insurance and any taxes you have. This doesn't include doing any types of renovations on your place because that is a "luxury."

Next, you want to take care of your transportation because if you don't have transportation, then you can't get to your job to make money. Transportation includes gas for your car, car payments (which I encourage you not to have!), and any maintenance. This of course does not include buying new rims for your ride or getting a lift put on with monster tires.

After transportation you want to take care of food. This is your basic groceries and does not include eating out. I know, it seems pretty harsh, but eating out is a "luxury" not a necessity.

And finally, you want to take care of clothing. Honestly, in America, we don't need any more clothes. I guarantee you could live on the clothes you currently have for another two to three years.

What about Leftovers?

Now, what if you have leftover money once you have paid your tithes and taken care of your basic necessities? That means you are doing something right! Now you have three options available: 1) Save, 2) Give, or 3) Spend.

Hopefully by this point you don't have any credit cards or debt, but if you do have some debt, there would be a fourth option: pay off debt. But for right now we will just stick with these three options.

1. Saving

It might seem like common sense to save money, but like the age-old quote reads, "the most uncommon thing is common sense." So if you have leftover money in your budget after your expenses are paid, a great place to start is saving that money.

Non Monthly Expenses

There will always be unexpected expenses that you didn't think about. It's like personal finance guru, Dave Ramsey, says, "I am actually amazed at how many people will go into debt for Christmas gifts. It's like Christmas snuck up on them again this year!"

So once you have done your simple budget, take some time and write out expenses that will be coming up in the future. Here are a few that you might not be thinking about: security deposits for rent and electricity, textbooks, traveling home, and that big spring break trip.

Every few months you want to look out at the next six months and see if there are any expenses that you need to save for. Here is another easy formula to help you figure out how much you need to be saving each month to reach your goal:

Total Amount Needed / Months Until Needed =

Amount to Save Each Month

For instance, if you are going to have to spend $800 on books in August and it is January, that would be 8 months away. So divide $800 by 8 months and you will need to be saving $100 each month to pay for your books.

Baby Emergency Fund

After you have figured out what all of your upcoming expenses are, it would be helpful to start saving money for an emergency fund. For some college students, your parents will serve as your emergency fund, but I think the emergency fund is a great first step towards financial independence. This fund will serve as a financial lifesaver for your college days and even after that. Many people depend on their credit cards for emergencies when all you really need to do is save $500 for when something goes wrong.

Granted, that amount probably won't be enough for the rest of your life, but it is definitely a great place to start while you are in college. Remember though, this is an *emergency* fund that should only be used for *emergencies*. That cute dress at Target or a new Xbox 360 game is not an emergency.

A blown tire or busted engine is an emergency, and you will be thankful you have $500 saved instead of a new purse or video game.

If you do have to spend that money on an emergency, it is okay. That is what the money is there for. Now your job is to refill your emergency fund and save up that $500 again.

2. Give a Little Bit

In an age of over-consumption, one of the best things for college students to learn in college is how to give. The tithe is what Randy Alcorn likes to call the "training wheels" of giving. It shouldn't be the last stop of your giving journey, only the beginning.

When I was in college I had more clothes than I knew what to do with. My junior year I started giving away a ton of my stuff, and I can honestly say that something inside of me broke. That whiney, little, spoiled brat of a kid that was hiding deep inside was exposed and dealt with. Giving released me from my selfishness, and it can for you, too.

Giving your stuff away is a great place to start, but it doesn't need to be the end of your giving. A lot of times it is easy to give away old clothes or junk that we don't want, but it is much harder to give away money, especially money that we could use to buy ourselves something.

The honest truth is that it is hard to part with your money. But when you realize that Psalm 24:1 ("the earth is God's and everything in it") is true, it becomes easier to give.

Instead of trying to figure out what you are going to do with your money, you get to talk with God and ask Him what He wants you to do with His money.

And the coolest part about giving is that we get to be a part of God showing His love and grace to people in a real and tangible way.

Several years back I was a leader in our church's college ministry. At the time I had a roommate who was also a leader in the college ministry. He had come to school without a car and would ride his long skate board to class everyday.

Our senior year a bunch of us decided that it was time for our friend to have a car. We all pitched in as much money as we could and bought a car for him. One night during our college service we stopped the service and took him outside to show him his new ride. The look on his face was absolutely priceless. At that moment he felt more loved than he ever had before in his life, and all because a bunch of college kids decided to give whatever they could.

3. Buying Stuff

Now, don't get me wrong. I am a real tight-wad, and I love to give, but I still really enjoy buying stuff. The key to buying things is to first disconnect from the idea that stuff will satisfy you or define you.

We are the most marketed-to country in the world and greed, materialism, and consumerism are no longer seen as vices but virtues. The key is to see stuff as just stuff and keep it in its rightful place. Don't let it consume you, and don't get caught up in the rat race of always trying to have more and more because no one ever wins that game. Be content with and enjoy the things that you already have.

You also have to realize that the only thing that can fully satisfy your need for love is Jesus Christ. Period. There is no amount of stuff that can ever satisfy you like Jesus can.

Secondly, the best way to pay for your things is by using cash. Study after study has shown that you will always spend more when you use a debit card or credit card. The reason is that it doesn't hurt to simply swipe a card. But it really hurts handing the cashier a bunch of twenty dollar bills that you spent the whole day working for.

You also have to realize that the credit card companies make it easy for you to use a credit card to "buy now and pay later" for a reason. The truth is you always end up paying more if you use a credit card instead of cash.

Let's say you decided to start paying for your stuff with a credit card rather than saving up and paying cash. If your credit card interest rate was 15% and you only paid the minimum payments, how much would it cost you? Take a look at figure 4.2.

At first the smaller things might not seem like that big of a deal to put on the credit card. You are only paying $26 more. But it never stops at just the smaller items, does it?

Let's keep going. If you decided to buy a new computer using a credit card, you would end up paying almost double for it.

And for the larger items like furniture, you might as well take some one hundred dollar bills and throw them down the drain.

Figure 4.2

Item	Original Cost	Cost Using Cash	Cost Using Credit Card	Difference Paid	Time to Pay Off
MP3 Player	$230	≤ $230	$256.94	$26.94	18 Months
New Laptop	$1,500	≤ $1,500	$2,854.18	$1,354.18	146 Months
New Sofa	$2,300	≤ $2,300	$4,654.29	$2,354.29	189 Months

Plain and simply, it doesn't make sense to use a credit card to buy things. The better choice is to save up little by little and pay cash for it.

One resource I have found that helps me save consistently for purchases is SmartyPig.com. This website asks you what your savings goal is and then each month automatically deducts it out of your checking account. Even better, each month you are able to earn a little bit of interest. This is a great tool for anyone who has trouble saving for those bigger purchases, which is everyone.

Who Cares?

Learning how to budget, give, and save might not seem very useful in your battle to survive college debt free, but with the average college student graduating with thousands of dollars in credit card debt, we have to realize that student loans are only one reason college students go into debt. It is a general lack of understanding how to manage money that is getting so many young people into trouble.

If you can learn how to manage the money that you earn through scholarships or even your work, you will be less likely to accumulate debt while you are in school.

The key when starting the process of implementing your cash flow plan is to keep it simple and actually do it. It won't help you to write out a budget on a piece of paper at the beginning of the month only to spend the rest of the month doing whatever you want. You have to stick to what you write on the piece of paper.

One of the best ways to help you in this process is to find an accountability partner who can hold your feet to the fire. Each month show them your budget and have them keep you accountable to doing what you said you were going to do.

Deep in the Heart of New Mexico

A few years back I had the opportunity to go on a camping trip to the beautiful mountains of New Mexico with my father-in-law, Steve, and my brother-in-law, J.J.

It was a glorious week-long trip of hiking some of the most beautiful terrain in all of America.

One day we decided that we wanted to go find a mountain-top lake called Joe Vigil Lake, which is known to have some of the best trout fishing in the Southwest. As I was fishing, J.J. and Steve decided to try and climb a few hundred feet to the top of the mountain. They left and I was able to enjoy the silence and solitude of being the only person fly-fishing a stunning mountain-top lake.

After a couple of hours of fishing, the silence was finally broken by thunder in the distance. If you have ever been on a hiking trip, you know that one of the worst places you can be during a lightning storm is on top of a mountain. It's even worse if you are terrified of lighting like I am. I packed up my stuff and started heading back up the hill to meet my father-in-law and brother-in-law as they were coming down. I ran into J.J. first and we started to head down a trail towards camp.

Steve was a little ways behind us and a few minutes into our trek back to camp we hear him yell, "Boys, I think camp is over this way." We didn't think too much about it, so we hopped on the different path and pushed it on home with thunder rolling in the background and lightning flashing all around us. As soon as we set foot into our campsite the downpour began. We made it safe and didn't get wet.

Great story, right?

Well, a few months later we were all sitting around reminiscing the trip and Steve said to me, "Josh, do you remember when we were up on top of that mountain in that thunder storm?"

"Of course I do! How could I forget?"

"Well, that path that you guys were on at first would have led you into some of the deepest and roughest terrain in all of New Mexico. You wouldn't have just ended up a few hundred yards off; you would have ended up miles and miles away from our camp. I decided to let you go down it for awhile to see if you would realize it was the wrong path, but eventually I realized you had no idea you were heading in the wrong direction."

The thing is, my father-in-law had hiked those mountains for 20 years. He knew where he was going and he knew what path he would take. I only knew what looked good at the time. My father-in-law knew the map, he knew the plan, and thankfully he told us the right way to go.

When you try to live your life without a map, you will choose what looks good at the moment and you will end up in the deepest and roughest terrain you can imagine. But the good news is that you now have that roadmap. Stick to it and you will eventually get to that cozy, campsite fire, and you won't be left out in the rain.

5
BUDGETING 2.0

Budgeting 2.0

The first step to a successful financial plan is establishing and consistently implementing a budget, and as we said in the previous chapter, the key to actually sticking to your budget is to keep it simple. Now that you understand the basics and know how to keep it simple, in this chapter I want to give you a few "extras" that will help you take your budgeting skills to the next level.

Distributed Budget

One of the best tools that I have seen help people who have a more complicated financial life is something called a distributed budget. If you have more than one paycheck coming in at different times in the month, a distributed budget becomes a lifesaver. Basically you are distributing all your expenses between your different checks.

At one time in our marriage, Jenny and I had seven checks coming in each month. That's right, SEVEN! At first it was brutal trying to figure out what bills we could pay and if we had enough money in our bank account. However, we started using the distributed budget and it brought so much peace of mind to our monthly budget meetings.

One of the benefits of doing a distributed budget is that it will save you from running into those dreaded NSF (not sufficient funds) charges.

All too often what will happen is you get one paycheck that has to last you until the 15th of the month. So you take that money and go out to eat, buy some groceries, and go to the movies, but on the 14th you have a bill that you have to pay. The bad news is that you have already spent all your money out of that paycheck.

Or your rent is $500, and your first check is $500, so there is no way that you can pay the entire rent payment with that one check and still put food on the table.

So what in the world are you supposed to do?

You have to do a distributed budget!

As you write out your budget each month, go ahead and put the due dates for each check out to the side. From here you can take out a different piece of paper and start your distributed budget. On the second sheet, create columns according to how many checks you have. Now using your first budget, distribute each of those expenses to its proper check.

Here is what it would look like if you had the following expenses: rent $500 due on the 1st, electricity $75 due on the 5th, gas $100, groceries $100, insurance $100 due on the 16th, savings $50 and tithes $100.

Figure 5.1	
Check #1 $500 on the 31st	Check #2 $500 on the 15th
Tithe -$50	Tithe -$50
Rent- $250	Rent- $250
Electricity - $75	Insurance - $75
Gas - $50	Gas - $50
Groceries - $50	Groceries - $50
Savings - $25	Savings - $25
Total Leftover - $0	Total Leftover - $0

For the first check, you will start by paying tithes right off the top. Next, since you can't pay the entire rent amount out of one check, you will split it between your two checks. So for the first check you will save $250. Next, since your electricity is due on the 5th, you will take the full $75 out of the first check. And finally for gas, groceries and savings, since there is no due date, you would simply distribute them to wherever you need them.

The distributed budget might take some time to get used to, but once you start implementing it you will feel much more at peace about having several checks coming your way.

Envelopes Aren't Just for Mail

Before there was email, we actually used these things called envelopes to mail letters. You may have only seen one of those envelopes when one of your blue-haired grandmas sent you a sweet birthday card but have you ever been around an old, blue haired lady when she is shopping at the grocery store? If not, next time you go to your local grocery store, watch an old lady check out. More than likely when it comes time to pay, she will reach into her purse, and take out this crazy thing called an "envelope" and pay for her groceries with this peculiar item known as "CASH." I know it might sound pre-Ice Age to use real money to pay for things and especially to use an envelope, but people have been doing it that way for years.

Don't be impressed by those people who whip out the platinum, silver, or titanium credit cards to pay for stuff. They're usually the ones with no real money, so they have to pay for things using what I like to call "monopoly money."

But if using cash and envelopes has worked for eighty years for those old ladies, there must be something to it. And what I have come to find out recently, is that there is actually this new craze going global called the (cue the Star Wars music) "envelope system." That's right, just like parachute pants and nasty mullets, using cash and envelopes is the new hip thing to do, and it won't make you hate yourself in twenty years when you're looking back through college pictures.

How Does the Envelope System Work?

So here is how it works: Let's take our previous expenses from the distributed budget. For everything that is a discretionary (big word, all it means is you can spend as much or as little at your discretion) spending category you are going to use the envelope system.

In our example the one discretionary spending category was groceries because although we have a budgeting amount for groceries we can actually spend more if we are using a credit card or debit card. So each paycheck we will get $50 in cash and put it in an actual envelope labeled "Groceries."

Here's the cool thing, whenever you go to the grocery store to buy groceries, guess how much you have to spend? That's right $50. Not fifty-ish. Fifty Dollars. And you can't spend anymore. The amazing thing about using the envelope system is that it makes you stick to what you have written down in your budget.

I would encourage you again to start simple. Don't try and do five envelopes your first month. Start with one, and groceries are usually a great one to start with. Once you feel comfortable with using one envelope, go ahead and start using two, then three, then four, and so on.

Currently, my wife and I use six envelopes – Groceries, Toiletries, Dining Out, Date Night, and Spending money for both of us. As I have said before, I was a drill sergeant with our money when we first were married, so when we first started implementing the envelope system, Jenny wasn't too sure what to think about it.

But to this day she would say that she absolutely loves using it because I can't say a thing about where she spends the money as long as she only spends what is inside of the envelope. So for those of you who might be worried about feeling constricted by the envelope system, it will actually give you more freedom because you have set boundaries to help you.

When Dreams Become Goals

The first two budget tools have been items that you can implement once you have already written your budget out. This next tool is one for you to work on before you have your budget set.

Study after study has shown that when you actually take the time to write out your goals, you are much more likely to attain them. I personally sit down each new season of the year and write out my goals for that next season.

As you write out goals for your life before, during and after school, be sure to include goals for your financial life. If you have been dating the same girl for a year or two, it might be wise to set a goal for saving up the money for an engagement ring and wedding. If you want that new car after college, instead of signing up for a car loan (which is a stupid idea), why not set a savings goal and pay cash for it?

If you are reading this book and haven't started school, then set a goal for how much you would like to have saved by your graduation date. Or better yet, figure out how much your education will cost and set a goal to have that amount saved by the beginning of each school year.

At the beginning of each of our coaching sessions, we start by asking people what their financial goals are. To this day I continue to be amazed when I meet with people and ask them what their goals are and they say, "We want to retire with a ton of money one day." My response is always, "That's great, what are you doing today to get there?" The dazed and confused look on their eyes is always a tell-tale sign that they have no idea!

So, the majority of our work is taking those pie-in-the-sky dreams and bringing them down to reality. That way, their bubbles aren't popped when they are 63-years old and expecting to retire in two years but they don't have any money in the bank.

The same is true for you as you are entering into or are already in college. If you want to graduate college debt free that is a great goal and I am all for it, but you have to put some meat on those bones to make sure that your dreams become reality.

That whole process of taking your dreams and bringing them down to real life and onto paper is what is known as setting goals.

You Sure Do Have Some S.M.A.R.T. Goals

Whenever I write out my financial goals, I use the well-known S.M.A.R.T. Goals Method. This method is the best way that I have found to bring my dreams and make them realistic and possible.

In the graph below, I have adjusted the "A" in the normal S.M.A.R.T. Goals format to be the "action" required to get to your goal.

Figure 5.2	
S.M.A.R.T. Goals	
Specific	What exactly are you going for? The specific part of the goal is the "What," "How," and "When." Instead of just wanting to be healthier, set a goal to lose 10 pounds by November 1st.
Measurable	How do you know if you are accomplishing your goal or have already accomplished it? If you haven't lost any weight by October 30th, then you probably aren't going to reach your goal!
Action	What action steps are you going to take to get to this goal? For example, do you need to become a member of the local gym to help you lose that weight?
Realistic	It might not be too realistic to plan to lose 10 pounds during a Thanksgiving holiday. As you are setting your goals ask yourself, "Can I really do this?"
Timely	What is the timeline for your goal? Have a specific end date in mind and write it down!

Good Goal vs. Bad Goal

Bad Goal: I want to buy a new car.

Good Goal: In two years, I will pay cash (up to $15,000) for a 2007 Honda Civic by saving and working extra jobs.

Do you see the difference? With a S.M.A.R.T. goal, you know exactly what you are shooting for, when you will get there, and what you are going to do to get there.

Backing Into Your Goals

Once you have written out your goals the next step is to say, "Okay, what do I need to do today to get to that goal?" If your goal is to buy a car in five years using cash, then you need to back yourself into that goal. No, I don't mean you need to back into someone, so insurance pays for your new car. What I mean is that you need to start with your goal and work back towards today.

That car is going to cost around $15,000, so you need to be saving $3,000 each year which means you need to be saving $250 each month. So today, you need to be putting a line in your budget that says, "New Car Fund" and putting $250 in that fund each month.

My freshman year of college I came in thinking that I was going to change the world. A friend was mentoring me at the time and helped me think through a plan of how I was going to accomplish such an extraordinary goal.

He started by saying, "Josh, what do you want people to say about you when you die?"

I thought to myself, "Well, that's a pretty morbid question to ask an 18 year old."

He continued, "If you were given the opportunity to listen in on what people said at your funeral, what would you want them to say?"

I thought for awhile, and then started to give him a list of my grand dreams. After I finished he asked, "Okay, what do you think you need to accomplish in the next 10 years to get there?" I gave him another grand list. "And what about the next five years?" he prodded. I mustered up another great list.

Finally he asked me the hardest question of all, "Josh, if you want to accomplish all this, what do you need to start doing tomorrow?"

Talk about Debbie Downer! Why couldn't this guy just let me keep dreaming about changing the world? So I told him, "I need to wake-up and spend time with God. I need to treat my roommate better. I need to read the Bible more."

My friend helped me take the huge dreams of my life and bring them back to reality. And how was I going to accomplish those huge dreams? By taking one, intentional step at a time in the right direction.

At first it might be difficult for you to be so specific with your goals, but as you begin to write out your goals more and more, you will realize that it becomes easier to put them into the S.M.A.R.T. goals format. You will also realize that you are accomplishing your goals more than your friends and colleagues because you have them WRITTEN DOWN.

Share Your Goals

I would also encourage you to share your goals with someone who can keep you accountable to them. If no one knows what you are shooting for, it is a lot easier to just give up on it. But if you have someone there beside you, pushing you, you are less likely to quit.

Last year one of our friends decided she was going to do her first sprint-triathlon. She trained for months and months and when it came down to the actual race day, we were all there to watch her achieve her goal.

As we talked with her before the race and asked her how she was feeling, she said that she was confident about the first two stages of the race, but the running portion was going to be extremely challenging. As soon as the race started, Jenny sent me back home to pick up her running shoes.

I got back to the race just in time to see our friend begin her transition to the running portion of the race.

I'm not too sure how legal it was, but as our friend hopped off of her bike and started running, Jenny was right there beside her. Over the next few miles, there were several times that our friend wanted to give up and walk, but she couldn't because Jenny was right there by her side encouraging her to finish and accomplish her goal.

A few hundred feet before the finish line, Jenny peeled off and watched as our friend ran across the finish line. Looking back, there is no way that our friend could have done it without Jenny there by her side cheering her on.

The same is true for your financial goals. There will be times when it is just too hard to save money each month or to make the necessary sacrifices to achieve your goals. When you share your goals with a trusted friend, they can push you back on track to make sure you reach your goals.

6
THE BEGINNING

So here we are: the final few pages. Growing up in church, I always looked forward to those glorious words that my pastor would utter at the end of his sermon, "And let me close with this..." Because I knew that he was about to 1) wrap-up his talk and I would soon be free to go eat lunch, and 2) give everyone a summary of everything we had just ignored for the past hour. So in the words of my old, country pastor, "let me close with this..."

Thresholds

When I married Jenny, the first thing I did when I brought her home after our honeymoon was pick her up in my arms and carry her across the threshold of our home. Husbands have been carrying their wives across the thresholds of their homes for hundreds of years. It is a powerful image showing that life is now different; we have crossed over into a new stage of our lives, and we will never be the same.

College is a major threshold in your life. You must choose to leave childish ways behind and become an adult. As you cross into adulthood, you must act like an adult. You must be responsible, a person of your word, hard working, diligent, and faithful. How you choose to live your life during college will greatly reflect how you live your life outside of college. Real life doesn't start when you get your first job or marry your sweetheart. Real life starts when you cross the threshold from being a child into being an adult. Now is the start of real life.

In the past few chapters, we have talked about a few simple ways for you to survive college debt free. We began by talking about one of the easiest and most straightforward of those ways being applying for and earning scholarships. It's free money and it is yours for the taking.

Secondly, we talked about the importance of working and how you really can pay for school with the money you earn from your jobs during summer and Christmas breaks.

And finally, we talked about the backbone of living a successful debt-free life: budgeting. We ended by giving you a few special tools for your tool belt to make you even more successful in your debt free journey.

You Are the Change

I have realized over the years that people love knowledge, but they hate to actually change their behavior. People, for the most part, want to be changed; they just don't want to change themselves. Instead, they want to be supernaturally or mysteriously changed in an instant by some outside force. Well, let me just tell you now, that will never happen! You are never mysteriously changed in an instant by some outside force.

For example, take one of my prayers that I prayed recently. For the most part, my personality tends to be one that hates details; therefore I am not thorough at all. I don't think about details and I would much rather rush through something without first thinking it through. I just want to get things done as quickly as possible. When it comes to marriage, this isn't always the best quality to have, especially when thoroughness is one of your wives best qualities. So one day I prayed, "God, could you help me be more thorough."

Now, what do you think God did to answer my request? Do you think He looked down from heaven, smiled and then sent a Holy lighting bolt of thoroughness to change me? Of course not! That would be too easy. And more than likely I would be thorough for about a week, then I would go right back to my old habits.

Instead, over the next month I had opportunity after opportunity to be thorough. It almost got to be annoying. It was like God was saying, "Josh, I'm not going to zap some thoroughness into you. I am going to give you opportunities to develop your thoroughness."

So every time I took the time to wash the dishes, or do the laundry, or vacuum the house, there was an opportunity staring me in the face to either be thorough or not to be thorough. Each time I scrubbed the dishes a little bit longer I was taking one step down the path towards thoroughness. I decided to take each opportunity that was given to me as choice to become more thorough. There was no magic formula for change, except to choose daily to change.

It Won't Be Easy, but It Will Be Worth It

Character change is not free and neither is college. If you want to graduate college debt free, you won't be given a free ride. The student loans won't magically disappear.

You will have to choose over and over and over and over to do whatever it takes to graduate college debt free.

It will be hard. It will be really, really hard. You will have to change your spending habits. You will have to change your work habits. You will have to search long and hard for scholarships. You will have to work longer and harder than you ever have in your life.

It will not be easy, but it will be worth it.

Run Fatboy!

A few months back, I was really feeling fat and out of shape. In high school I played a bunch of sports, and I would consider myself an athletic person. With the arrival of our first baby, normal life stopped for awhile and my belly began to get huge. After a couple of months of living the baby life, I looked down and someone had replaced my six-pack with something that resembled my grandpa's belly. It was time for a change.

I decided at that exact moment that I was going to lose weight. But the next few nights I continued to eat the same things for dinner and instead of going for a run, I just sat on the couch and watched my favorite television shows. And guess what, my grandpa's belly was still there, and it was continuing to grow. Doing the same thing as before didn't change anything. I had to do something radically different. I actually had to suck it up and pay for a membership to the YMCA.

But just buying a membership to the YMCA wasn't enough; I actually had to go. And I couldn't just go, I had to run and I had to work out. But then when I got home, I couldn't just eat the same old stuff. I had to change my eating habits, and our family had to change what groceries we bought.

You see, it took me changing absolutely everything to get the results that I wanted. If I would have stayed on that same path, I would have looked down in 40 years and not been able to see my toes.

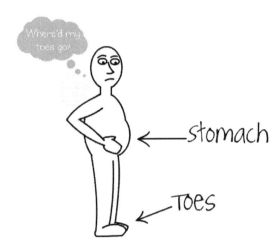

I didn't really want that. I want to be healthy. I want to live to watch my kids grow up. I want to grow old with my wife. And, most importantly, I want to see my toes!

So I had to change my game plan.

The same is true for you. If you want to make it through college debt free and start your adult life on a solid financial foundation, you can't live like all the other college kids. You have to be different, radically different.

Take some time now and decide what that means for you. Do you need to start applying for more scholarships?

Do you need to start doing a monthly cash flow plan? Or do you need to actually start working?

Whatever it is, let me encourage you to start doing it today. Don't wait a few months until it is too late. Start today implementing those easy ideas that can and will have life-altering impact.

The Two Houses

In the Bible in the book of Matthew, Jesus tells a parable about two people who built two different houses. You have probably heard it all before, but let me remind you of the story. It goes a little like this, "Therefore everyone who hears these words of mine and puts them into practice is like a wise man who built his house on the rock. The rain came down, the streams rose, and the winds blew and beat against that house; yet it did not fall, because it had its foundation on the rock. But everyone who hears these words of mine and does not put them into practice is like a foolish man who built his house on sand. The rain came down, the streams rose, and the winds blew and beat against that house, and it fell with a great crash."

The two houses in this story probably looked a lot alike. They probably had a nice overall structure and feel. The builders probably put an immense amount of energy and thought into every square inch of the house. The problem wasn't the detail of the house, or even the foundation of the house. The problem was where they put the house.

One guy decided to put his house on a rock and one guy decided to put his house on sand. Easy enough. But what does Jesus say that rock is? Jesus? No, the rock is the act of putting into practice what they have been hearing Jesus teach the whole time.

Both guys had the opportunity to choose to put into practice what they heard. One obeyed and he was left standing. One didn't care too much, and he was washed away.

My prayer for you is that you would be the one who hears what I have been talking about these past few chapters and doesn't just think that it's a good idea or a funny book. My hope and prayer is that you would hear these words and put them into action, so that when the storms of life do come, you will be left standing with a house that was built on the rock. God bless.

APPENDIX A:
PLANNING AHEAD

As I mentioned in the book, one of the best ways for you to pay for your college education is by getting a head start while you are still in high school. Many high school students don't realize that putting in the extra effort to study hard and prepare for their PSAT or SAT and ACT will pay off immensely down the road

One of the often over-looked and undervalued tests is the PSAT. Many students only see this as a test that helps them prepare for the SAT. The PSAT does serve as a great preparation tool, but students can also use their high scores to qualify for a National Merit Scholarship.

Many times students can receive a full ride or full tuition for either being a National Merit Semi-Finalist or National Merit Finalist.

For more information on the PSAT and the National Merit Scholarship Corporation, please visit www.CollegeBoard.com and/or www.NationalMerit.org.

APPENDIX B:
THE BEST FIRST OPTION

Sometimes the worst news that I have to give a college student is that they shouldn't attend their dream college (at least the first couple years). For some students, the best first option for college is to attend a junior college or their local community college.

These smaller schools often offer a great education for a fraction of the price. They are also great "proving grounds" for those students who didn't have stellar academic records during their high school days.

If you are diligent to make great grades at a smaller college, you will be more eligible to receive larger scholarships from the "major universities."

It might not sound like the best news, but often times attending a smaller school at a fraction of the price is the best option for some students.

HELPFUL RESOURCES

Don't Get Suckered Book

Suckered. Thousands of young college students are suckered each year to believe that the only way for them to graduate college is by taking on a mountain of debt, then they spend the next ten, twenty, or event thirty years paying for the most expensive piece of paper they have ever received. But isn't there a better way? Yes! In "Don't Get Suckered," Josh Lawson explains in a fresh, funny, and insightful way how college students can walk across the stage on graduation day DEBT FREE.

by Josh Lawson, 117 pages: **$11.97**.
Special Price! 20% off ten or more:$9.58 each or 40% off a case of 70 books: $7.18 each

Don't Get Suckered Audio Book – Coming Soon!

For your home or car. Read by author Josh Lawson. The full CD set: $24.97.

Check out our web site
www.financesrestored.com
for more helpful resources and to connect with others.

MORE HELPFUL RESOURCES

Where to Find Scholarship Information

FAFSA – www.fafsa.ed.gov

Kaarme – www.kaarme.com/find_scholarships

Fastweb – www.fastweb.com

Financial Planning Help

Financial Peace University®

FPU is a 13-week, life-changing program that empowers and teaches you how to make the right money decisions to achieve your financial goals and experience a total money makeover. Each lesson is taught via video by Dave Ramsey, a Christian financial counselor, bestselling author, and radio show host.

www.DaveRamsey.com/FPU

The Total Money Makeover – Dave Ramsey

An updated, expanded version of Ramsey's first book about overcoming debt and managing personal finances, this edition boasts new chapters on the relationship between money matters and family matters.

www.DaveRamsey.com

The Treasure Principle- Randy Alcorn

Randy Alcorn's *The Treasure Principle (Discovering the Secret of Joyful Giving)* introduces readers to a revolution in material freedom and radical generosity that will change lives around the world.

www.epm.org

Money, Possessions and Eternity- Randy Alcorn

It's time to rethink our perspectives on money and possessions. In this thoroughly researched and extensively updated classic, Randy Alcorn shows us how to view them accurately—as God's provision for our good, the good of others, and his glory.

www.epm.org

Work Help

48 Days to the Work You Love - Dan Miller

48 Days to the Work You Love, is not so much about finding a new job as it is learning about who we are really called to *be* in relation to our vocation-whatever shape that career may take in these changing times.

www.48days.com

ABOUT THE AUTHOR

Josh Lawson serves as the director of Community Restoration at Antioch Community Church in Waco, Texas. He is passionate about seeing families set free from the burden of debt and financial stress, so that they are free to walk in the freedom that Christ has for them.

In the past three years, he and his team have seen over 450 families attend Dave Ramsey's *Financial Peace University* and over 250 families have received one-on-one financial coaching.

In his spare time Josh enjoys reading, fly fishing, woodworking, and going on walks with his family. Josh and his wife, Jenny, live with their son, Asher, in Waco, Texas, where they are members of Antioch Community Church.

If you are interested in learning more about his ministry, having Josh come and speak, or would like to contact us for any other reason, we would love to hear from you!

Please send all requests to:
Josh Lawson
505 N. 20th
Waco, Texas 76707

Made in the USA
Charleston, SC
30 September 2011